C000212443

THE Somerset & Dorset Line From Above

Bath to Evercreech Junction

THE Somerset & Dorset Line From Above

Bath to Evercreech Junction

KEVIN POTTS | Aerial Photography ALLAN BURNEY and MARK WAGNER AVIATION IMAGES
Additional Colour Images MARK B WARBURTON

First published 2013

ISBN 978 0 7110 3755 7

All rights reserved. No part of this book may be reproduced or transmitted in any form or by any means, electronic or mechanical, including photocopying, recording, scanning or by any information storage and retrieval system, on the internet or elsewhere, without permission from the Publisher in writing.

© Ian Allan Publishing Ltd 2013

Published by Ian Allan Publishing

an imprint of Ian Allan Publishing Ltd, Hersham, Surrey KT12 4RG.

Printed in Estonia.

Visit the Ian Allan Publishing website at *www.ianallanpublishing.com*

Copyright
Illegal copying and selling of publications deprives authors, publishers and booksellers of income, without which there would be no investment in new publications. Unauthorised versions of publications are also likely to be inferior in quality and contain incorrect information. You can help by reporting copyright infringements and acts of piracy to the Publisher or the UK Copyright Service.

PICTURE CREDITS The aerial photographs in this book were taken by Allan Burney and Mark Wagner and are the copyright of Aviation Images. The historical photographs were taken by Mark B. Warburton and are the copyright of his estate.

FRONT COVER MAIN IMAGE
The viaduct at Midford - *see* page 34
FRONT COVER BOTTOM IMAGE
9F No 92001 on the Somerset & Dorset, August 1962. *Photo by Ivo Peters, copyright Julian Peters*
BACK COVER Charlton Viaduct - *see* page 98
PAGE 1 Five Arches - *see* page 58
PAGE 2 Midsomer Norton Station - *see* page 62
PAGE 3 Chilcompton Station - *see* page 72
RIGHT Radstock - *see* page 52

Contents

The Somerset & Dorset Line from Above – The Story of an Idea

Every railway lover will have his or her favourite railway; invariably also this choice will have been formed during childhood. This will probably be based upon one or two criteria – it may have been geographically close to one's early home, or possibly the line that was used for holidays or travel to school.

Ask a group of individuals to define their favourite railway line and the answer will be subjective, but ask the same question as to which are the most popular lines generally and one name will occur over and over again, the Somerset & Dorset. In the next breath will come a discourse on how this (or any other) route should never have been closed, how useful it would be now, and even the idea of rebuilding the route in the form it appeared years ago.

But all this is pure nostalgia. Using the S&D as the example, closure occurred nearly half a century ago, in a different age when priorities were also perceived to be different. Since then we have evolved as a society. Times have indeed changed, but regardless as to how and why the line was condemned back in 1966, it would simply not be a financially feasible proposition to restore everything from Bath Green Park south through Evercreech and Templecombe to Bournemouth. That is not to say there might not well be a compelling argument for a railway link in the general area but to resurrect the S&D in its entirety is unlikely ever to occur.

As an iconic railway the S&D had it all, beautiful countryside to traverse, main line trains which were often double headed, quaint branch lines leading off it, local services, a unique mixture featuring a blend of LMS, Southern and in later years BR steam, steep gradients where men and machine might be pitted against nature and as an added bonus the enthusiastic following generated through the likes of the imagery of Ivo Peters, and reminiscences of men like Donald Beale and Peter Smith. Small wonder the list of books published on or featuring the S&D must surely be approaching three figures.

So why this new pair of books? (Volume 2 covering the line from Evercreech to Bournemouth and the branches will be published in July 2013.) The answer is simple: here is the opportunity to look at the railway in a totally new way. We know what we have attempted has never been done before featuring the S&D; indeed to the best of our knowledge only one similar title has ever been published, a delightful little paperback *Flying the Lynton & Barnstaple*, produced by the L&B Association and now out of print – but well worth tracking down a copy if you can.

Seen from the air a railway, whether operational or moribund, takes on a totally new perspective. Aerial images, whether in oblique or vertical form, of places we may be totally conversant with from the ground immediately seem unfamiliar seen in a different context within the landscape. Notwithstanding having been impressed by the L&B volume, in considering a similar approach for the S&D we were immediately faced with the problem of the best method of both presenting and then describing what had once been a major railway but which in many areas had not just been decimated but its remnants built over so as to be unrecognisable from ground level.

Much discussion took place, but in the end we realised the only true way of assessing the potential was to attempt an aerial sortie, notwithstanding the obvious costs involved. Here we were slightly disadvantaged compared with our friends at the L&B; we could hardly ask a favour over a route 70+ miles long, and that excludes the branches. Nonetheless, the decision was made, the cost authorised and developments were awaited with bated breath.

We were not to be disappointed even if it took a little time to go ahead with photographing the complete route. Here the British climate also took a part. The cameraman advised us that ideally the low level aerial photography had to be accomplished by July – this being for reasons of light. But then the vagaries of the summer of 2012 took hold and for days the crew were grounded due to low cloud. Remember 2012 – almost the wettest year on record?

But perhaps the historic gods of the S&D were indeed once again keen on their railway appearing in the limelight, for a weather 'window' opened up and a photographic survey of the complete route was finished with little time before the clouds rolled in again. (If we are to repeat the exercise for another line in 2013 we can only hope that it must surely be our turn for a proper summer.)

It took several days for the photographs to be sorted and then numbered in sequential order – there were several hundred. It might be thought there would be no need for this number of images but considering the complexity of some locations, Bath being the obvious example, plus others like the entrance to the tunnels, viaducts, station remains etc, we had to ensure that every important feature was recorded. Then came the difficult task of assessing each as to suitability. We quickly gave up; this was a role best suited to the author, and who better than a man who was not only an enthusiast himself but also an experienced fixed-wing pilot and so able to interpret the various features, placing these in their context on the ground.

Kevin Potts is a remarkable man*: professional in his approach, and enthusiastic in the extreme, but a man who was also concerned as to his ability to produce what we had asked of him. More than once he came back to ask for clarification; we reassured him, confident we had made the right choice. When he submitted his finished draft we knew immediately he had been the correct choice. He had provided the perfect balance between history and modern day – aided we are told by several visits to various hostelries on the route south of Bath to his own home in Bournemouth.

Matters now took an unexpected turn. We were quietly confident the aerial images and captions were strong enough on their own, the idea being to supplement these on occasions with black and white photography and of course maps. But then enter upon the scene our friends at the Stephenson Locomotive Society. In conversation with the SLS Librarian Gerry Nichols, we happened one day to mention the proposed new book, whereupon we were informed of possible access to a new and unpublished collection of S&D colour material from the camera of the late Mark Warburton. Discussion with Mrs Margaret Warburton followed and we are delighted to acknowledge her assistance with the project.

Fortunately, Mark was one those men who kept meticulous records of his photographic excursions; these included dates and locomotive details plus on occasions actual train workings. Aided by Mark's note books, Gerry was able to convert these into informative and detailed captions of the railway as it appeared in the early to mid 1960s, not in any way intending to create a 'then and now' book but instead a new look at the present, comparing it with a glimpse of the past.

*As a raconteur of his experiences on the modern day rail network he is probably without equal.

Producing an introduction to a new type of railway book is not easy. So many books, some great, some good, some not so good, some frankly awful, have appeared over the years. Although each will have been prefaced with words intended to describe what follows sometimes such words almost serve to be an excuse for what follows; that is certainly not the intention now. Instead we seek to explain the rationale for a book that is altogether different and which we intend to be the first in a sequence.

Success should also not be judged purely on commercial grounds – although clearly the investor expects some return – but we believe what we set out to achieve has been accomplished. Like many projects it has evolved; we could not have foreseen the opportunity that was presented with the inclusion of Mark's colour views, but they were clearly far too good to be ignored.

Closed lines in the south of England have generally not fared well compared with those in areas such as rural Wales, the north of England or Scotland. An increasing population, ever more motor vehicles and demands for housing plus the associated services to serve these groups have meant that what are nowadays termed 'brown field sites' are eagerly snapped up for commercial or private development. Often all that remains are a few words at the entrance to a group of houses, such as 'Station Road' or 'The Sidings'. Perhaps the most poignant of these was the pub sign at Evercreech which, post 1966, changed its name from 'The Railway Inn' to 'The Silent Whistle'. Indeed since 1966 great swathes of the S&D have disappeared under concrete or brickwork, stations have been demolished, track bed turned into roads, ballast into paths or in some places simply returned to farmland. In isolation it might just be possible to restore a small section of the line, but as discussed earlier, in its entirety I think not.

Even so there are splashes of the old being resurrected. Midsomer Norton, Shillingstone and the Gartell Light Railway near Templecombe are obvious examples, although similar attempts at Radstock and Midford were sadly doomed to failure. It is also not just in the form of a resurrected railway that the route may be useful. Sections of trackbed have, or will be, converted into cycle and walking paths including even access through the notorious Devonshire and Combe Down tunnels near Bath.

Ian Allan Publishing has plans to extend this style of project to cover other iconic and long lamented lines. Much will of course depend upon the summer of 2013, assuming it is considered suitable for flying. So if you see a light aircraft overhead somewhere later this year … you might care to view the catalogue for the year 2014 and beyond.

NICK GRANT
Ian Allan Publishing Ltd

Aerial Photography

Somerset & Dorset prints for sale!

High quality prints of the air-to-ground images featured within this book are available to purchase.
For details, please see www.aviation-images.com

The Somerset & Dorset Railway

The Somerset & Dorset Joint Railway was renowned for the variety and beauty of its scenery but its topography presented extreme challenges to its builders and the enginemen who worked on the line. The first section of the line from Bath to Evercreech, covered in this volume, was particularly demanding. The map right shows the whole route and as can be seen the first section featured numerous tunnels and viaducts in quick succession. As the line crossed the Mendip hills the line reached a height of 811ft (247m) above sea level at Masbury, the severity of the climb evident in the gradient profile below. The photographs that follow in this book will – we hope – remind the reader of just how attractive the route of the Somerset & Dorset was but are also a tribute to the human endeavour that created the railway and made it work for 100 years.

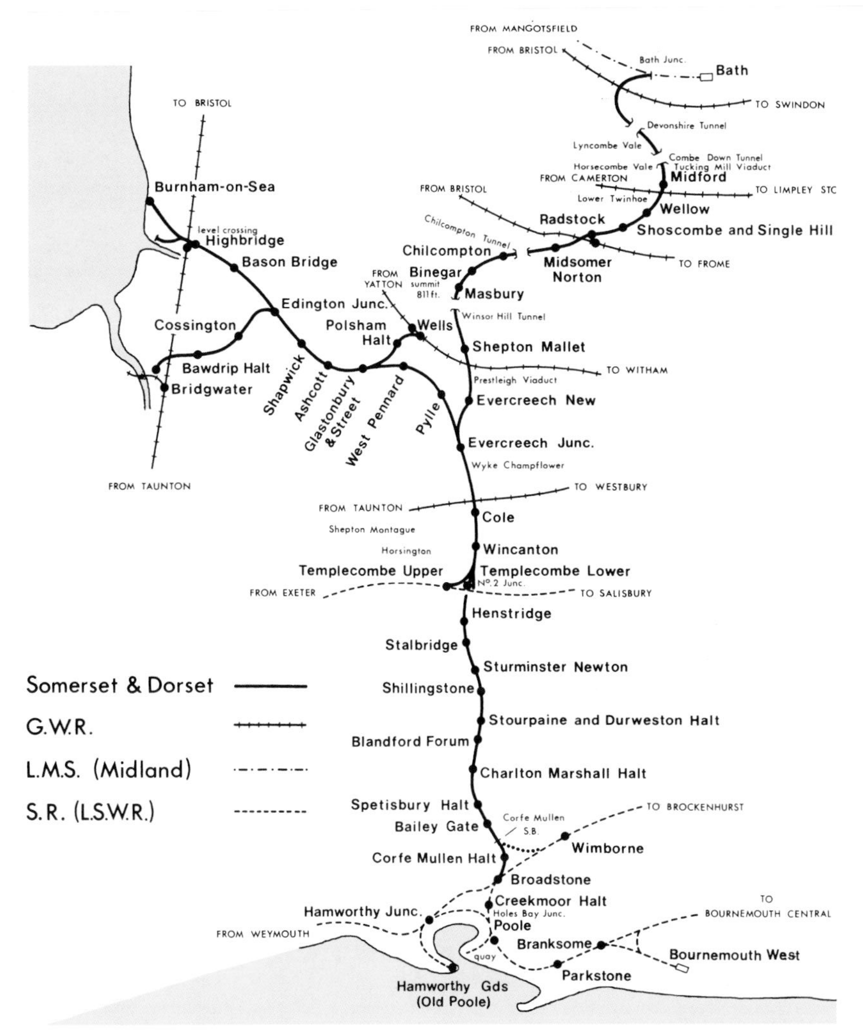

BELOW Map and gradient profile reproduced from *An Historical Survey of the Somerset & Dorset Railway* by C.W. Judge and C.R. Potts, OPC, 1979/1988.

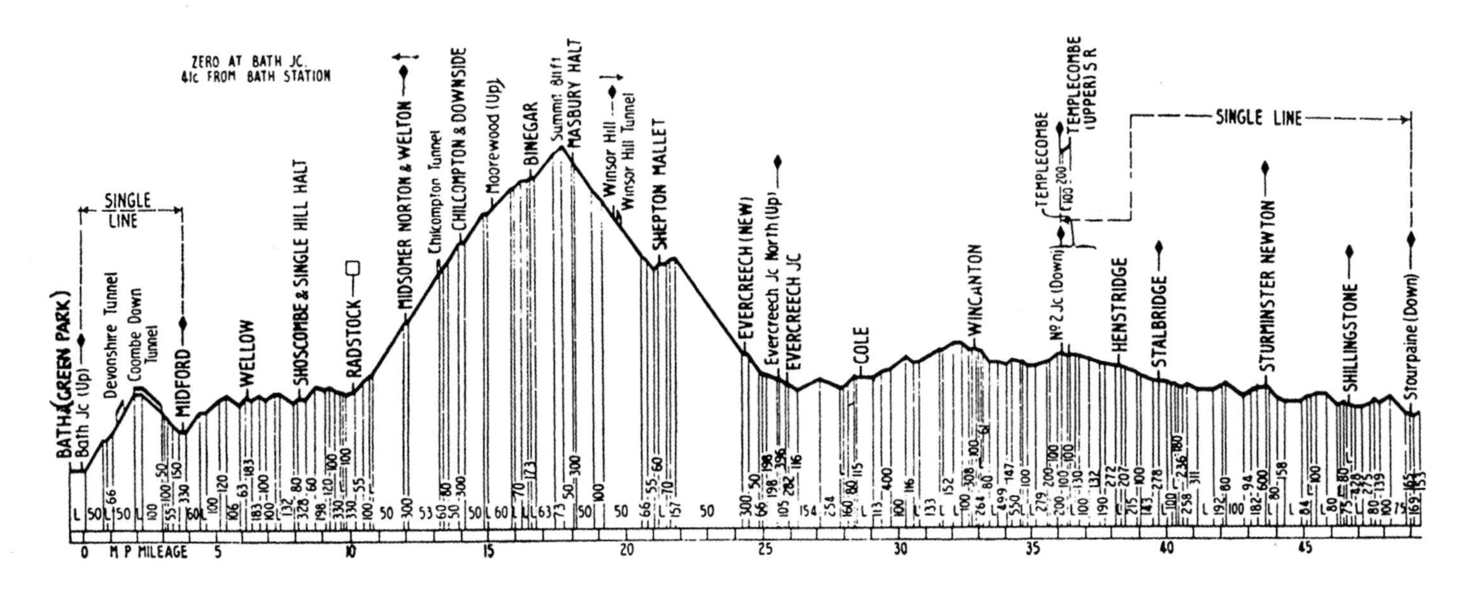

Bath Green Park

ABOVE Looking from the south east the only railway infrastructure that is immediately apparent today is the current mainline slicing diagonally across the picture. Bath Spa station is just out of sight to the right and to the left the line continues onwards towards Bristol. The tree lined banks mark the path of the River Avon with the train shed roof of the former Bath Green Park station still standing magnificently to the north. Seemingly isolated from its railway past and with little obvious clue in its surroundings, this remains as a monument to the Somerset & Dorset Joint Railway.

FACING PAGE Once again the River Avon can be used to draw the eye toward Bath Green Park station buildings. The glass fronted station façade can just be seen. It is more difficult to trace the path of the trackbed once the station limits are left behind but the sites of the former gasholders in the lower left of the picture provide a helpful landmark. The line crossed the River Avon immediately after leaving the station and continued west for half a mile along former Midland Railway metals running level and just to the north of the row of Victorian houses in the centre of the picture. It then branched off to the south at Bath Junction, just to the right of the site of the two smaller gasholders.

The frontage of the 1870 Midland Railway Bath station is seen on 19 April 1965 prior to a journey on the 9.53am as far as Templecombe. The Green Park name dates from 1951 to avoid confusion with the Great Western station which was known as Bath Spa from 1949. A period selection of a Standard Vanguard and Austin A35 flank the No Parking sign in front of the station while the photographer's VW Beetle is visible on the side road to the right hand side of the building.

'9F' No 92210 draws into Bath Green Park station with the Bournemouth West to Derby train on the morning of Saturday 4 August 1962. The arrival is observed by the crew of No 75073 which had arrived earlier with a local train from Templecombe and was waiting for a path to the shed. No 92210 still carries the 82F Bath Green Park shedcode which it would lose the following week when it was exchanged for 92220 *Evening Star*.

FACING PAGE Viewed from the north a closer examination of the former station surroundings illustrates just how confined the site was. Bath Green Park remains in use today as an indoor market with the station pedestrian entrance to the left of the glazed roof. Immediately to the right of the train shed is Sainsbury's supermarket, the car park occupying much of the area outside. Two parallel bridges carry the trackbed over the river, the closer of the two having been converted for foot traffic. The larger car park and building in the centre of the picture occupy the site of both the S&D and Midland engine sheds. (With a prevailing south westerly wind, the occupants of Norfolk Crescent must have appreciated the atmosphere surrounding a busy steam shed!) The other side of the central collection of trees formed the site of the Goods Yard and coal sidings.

ABOVE Another view of Bath Green Park station. The former double railway bridge carrying the tracks over the River Avon stands out clearly, as does the lower road bridge on Midland Bridge Road. The station was always limited by platform length; even after extension towards the river bridge the northern platform could still only accommodate a maximum of nine bogies. Upon crossing the river, the site occupied by the former engine sheds is now taken up by a retail park and car parks immediately above the row of trees. The area below formed the goods yard. Interestingly, the road crossing the river on the former rail bridge is named Stanier Road and leads into Pines Way. Provision was made for waterfront sidings running on the western bank of the river to enable transhipment of goods.

ABOVE Pulling back to give a wider view of Bath's south western quadrant, the Royal Crescent stands out in the top left of the picture. Tracing the path of the former trackbed beyond the engine shed area, the line ran out to the west. It passed just to the north of the row of houses (Victoria Buildings) seen to the left of shot and just below the building site by the river. Running parallel to Lower Bristol Road the line continued level before leaving the Midland in a sweeping curve to the left and beginning the climb out of Bath.

FACING PAGE Looking from the north, Victoria Buildings can be seen just off the centre of the picture. The gasholders to the right mark the site of Bath Junction. The Somerset & Dorset diverged to the left at a point just above the gasholders, entering a single line section and beginning a gruelling 1 in 50 climb for two miles to the mouth of Combe Down Tunnel. The line crossed Lower Bristol Road on a skew bridge (long gone) before traversing a complete semi-circle to reappear in the picture as a line of trees visible in the upper right section of the photograph.

No 53804 couples on to its five coaches for a Stephenson Locomotive Society Special to Templecombe and back on Sunday 11 September 1960. W. A. Camwell brought his SLS Special headboard which the engine carried when it left. The platform ramp to the left of the front of the engine illustrates how short the platforms were at Bath Green Park station due to the proximity of the bridge over the River Avon and the siding adjacent to the Bonded Store.

No 76015 departs from Green Park with a Bournemouth train on Saturday 10 April 1965, passing the engine sheds on the left (the wooden building of the SDJR shed is visible but the stone Midland shed is hidden behind the locomotive) and pannier tank No 3681 on the Bath Goods pilot duty.

An elevated view of Bath taken from the south. With the benefit of careful study some of the features highlighted in other shots should enable the reader to identify Bath Green Park station although little else of Somerset & Dorset relevance is visible. The current main line to the west runs across the bottom of the picture whilst Royal Crescent to the left hand side demonstrates why the city is still such a tourist attraction.

A final overall view of Bath taken from the west. The former terminus at Bath Green Park sits in the centre of the picture. The railway, as already described, would have passed over the river before running out of view just to the north of Lower Bristol Road. The beginning of the climb out of Bath would have taken it over today's existing mainline at right angles before continuing in a sweeping curve to the south east towards Devonshire Tunnel. Of interest, Bath Spa station can be seen on the curve to the top right of the picture with the newly regenerated city centre shopping area immediately to the left.

Midland Main Line

ABOVE Bath Junction, taken from the north. At this point trains for the south and Bournemouth entered Somerset & Dorset metals. It also marked the start of a two-mile climb at 1 in 50 and the beginning of the single line section to Midford. The line ran between Lower Bristol Road and the gasholders. Immediately above the gasometer site is a crossroads; the line swinging over this on a skew bridge to continue along the grassy former trackbed visible beyond. The bridge has gone but the white building on the far side of the crossroads – the 'Royal Oak' public house – remains.

FACING PAGE This view, taken from virtually overhead Bath Junction, shows the sweeping curve of the line as it reverses direction in the bottom right of the picture. It crosses the Western mainline to Bristol, Exeter and the southwest before continuing the climb towards Devonshire tunnel. The gradient that so many trains struggled up (and down!) is marked by the avenue of trees and now forms a footpath. Housing estates have expanded on either side of the line.

No 75072 swings on the Somerset & Dorset line at Bath Junction on 10 April 1965 and the signalman prepares to hand over the single line tablet to the fireman. The Whitaker automatic tablet exchange apparatus can be seen in the foreground but this engine which had worked up on the 12.00 from Templecombe did not have the catcher fitted. Permanent Way Trolley B11W (Wickham Works No 6651) was delivered new to Bristol in 1953 and was on the SDJR from at least 1960 working between Shepton Mallet and Bath. It was withdrawn in 1970 and sold to the Dart Valley Railway.

Bath City Overview

One of the joys of flying as a professional pilot is access to some stunning aerial views such as the one that the crew filming the route were able to capture here. It shows Bath from the south and is included as a panoramic picture that highlights Bath and the picturesque surroundings the city sits within. The former Great Western mainline runs across the bottom of the shot but I will leave it to the reader to pick out features previously identified that belong to the Somerset & Dorset.

Devonshire – Combe Down Tunnel

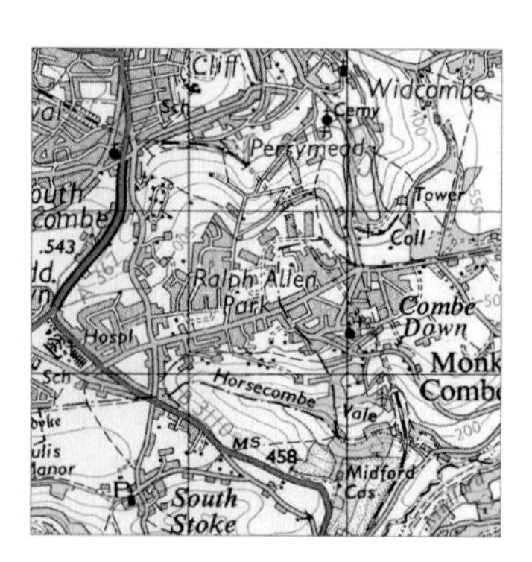

ABOVE With the camera positioned high above Devonshire Bank a panoramic view of the full 1½-mile climb from Bath Road Junction to Lyncombe Vale can be seen. Starting from the familiar reference point of the gasholders (upper right) the sweeping curve of the line is marked out by the row of trees until it passes under the present day A367 in the lower left of the picture. Known as Devonshire Tunnel, the southern portal opens out into the picturesque Lyncombe Vale marked by the wooded area at the bottom of the shot.

FACING PAGE Repositioning the camera further to the south and zooming in towards Devonshire Bank itself, the line is now straddled by housing estates. The former trackbed has been converted into a foot and cycle path. The end of the treeline towards the bottom of the picture marks the northern portal of Devonshire Tunnel. Apart from a brief level section towards the midpoint of the bank, the climb is an unrelenting 1 in 50 up to and through Devonshire Tunnel and into the Lyncombe Vale beyond.

Will it fit? The fireman of No 92233 has done the hard work and takes a breather as the single bore of Devonshire tunnel approaches. The load of the 7.35am Nottingham to Bournemouth West 1091 on Saturday 1 September 1962 was only eight coaches and so no pilot was needed over the Mendips.

LEFT Often, when faced with a photograph taken today of yesterday's railway landscape, it can be difficult to pick out features which at one time seemed so distinctive. The lower section of Devonshire Bank with its curve set high on an embankment has been featured in countless photographs of the Somerset & Dorset. Now overgrown with vegetation it is only from the air that the picture becomes clear. Some of the original over and underbridges on the climb remain. Others, previously demolished, have been replaced by new structures such as the modern footbridge over Monksdale Road. This can be seen in the lower section of the picture.

ABOVE Another shot of the new footbridge at Monksdale Road is included here just for those who have no concerns about vertigo! As the line passes over the bridge from right to left the climb out of Bath recommences, initially at 1 in 66 before steepening to 1 in 50 once more.

Lyncombe Vale between the Devonshire and Combe Down tunnels is not greatly disturbed as Nos 53808 and 73047 drift down the 1 in 50 with the 9.25am Bournemouth to Liverpool and Manchester service on Saturday 1 September 1962. No 53808, which is still with us and based on the West Somerset Railway, was attached at Evercreech Junction for the climb across the Mendips.

Devonshire Tunnel is 440 yards long. It was built with an extremely narrow bore, taking the line under the road (A367) and built up area to the left of the picture and emerging in the Lyncombe Vale. Access to the tunnel portal was not possible for years since the line was landscaped and partly backfilled to prevent this. It is only at the time of writing (2013) that the ability of being able to traverse the entire route from Bath Road Junction to Midford (via both tunnels and Tucking Mill viaduct) is becoming reality once more. The Two Tunnels Project is aiming to see the trackbed regenerated for recreational use adding to those sections already in use as described elsewhere. Looking further down the bank to the right hand side of the picture, the attractive three arch bridge over the present day Hiscocks Drive still stands.

Tucking Mill Viaduct

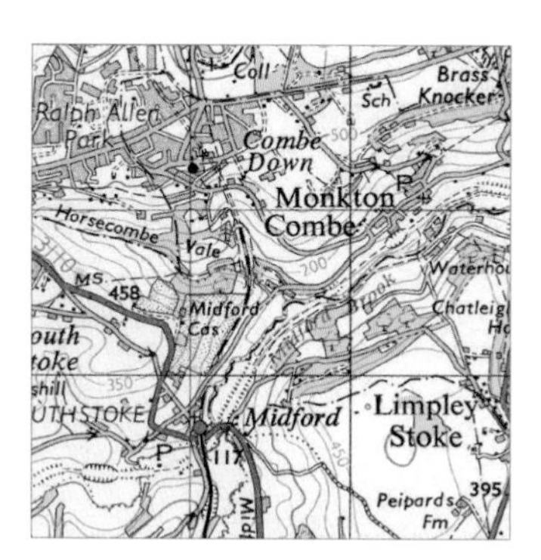

FACING PAGE Southbound trains from Bath entered Combe Down Tunnel two miles after passing over Bath Junction. At 1,829 yards long it was another narrow bore, unventilated tunnel although at least the gradient changed in their favour shortly after passing through the northern portal. Although only a short distance from Bath, already the scenery has changed dramatically. Emerging into the Horscombe Vale the line now runs through some of the most attractive and photographed scenery on the route as it meanders downhill towards Midford. The picture shows the line emerging from Combe Down tunnel in the top right of the shot and sweeping gracefully over Tucking Mill viaduct. Once again, lineside vegetation has overgrown much of the track formation.

ABOVE Looking from the northeast, the line sweeps out of the cutting from Combe Down Tunnel and over Tucking Mill viaduct. The small lake/reservoir to the left has been used for fishing. The viaduct is intended to form part of the recreational route allowing cyclists and walkers to pass through both tunnels and on through the Horscombe Vale to Midford.

A late afternoon train, possibly the local to Binegar from Bath, hauled by No 82004, has just left Combe Down Tunnel and makes its way across Tucking Mill viaduct on Tuesday 16 June 1964. This viaduct was originally built for single track and widened in 1891 as a first step to alleviating the bottleneck of the single line from Bath Junction to Midford. The economics of doubling the two tunnels prevented fulfilment of the scheme.

FACING PAGE Tucking Mill viaduct was a popular setting for photographs taken on the line before closure. An impressive eight-arch structure, it rises 63 feet above the valley below and extends for 96 yards. The viaduct was widened in 1891-2 to accept double track. This never happened and the double track section of the line ended on Midford viaduct further to the south. Today, the airborne camera struggles to capture the full extent of the viaduct with trackside vegetation encroaching upon the structure.

ABOVE With Tucking Mill viaduct in the lower left of the picture, the line continues to meander southwards towards Midford, seen towards the top of the shot. Midford Castle sits on the high ground to the right. This panoramic view also shows the GWR Camerton–Limpley Stoke branchline running along the valley bottom and converging on the Somerset & Dorset at Midford. It crossed under the line at Midford viaduct.

Midford Station and Viaduct

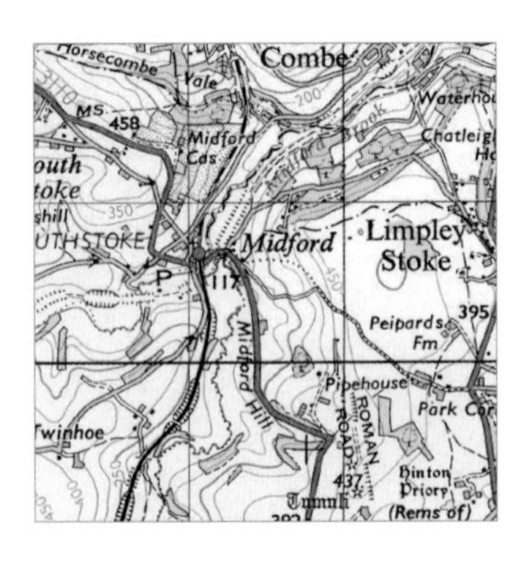

ABOVE Viewed from the southeast, the site of Midford station and viaduct stands out in the centre of the picture. The GWR branchline from Limpley Stoke, completed in 1910, cuts in from the right as it follows the path of Midford Brook. It then passed beneath Midford viaduct before tracking out towards the top of the picture. This crossing of Somerset & Dorset with Great Western metals was, of course, immortalised in the classic 1952 Ealing comedy *The Titfield Thunderbolt*. Descending from Combe Down Tunnel the line meanders from top right to bottom left of our view.

FACING PAGE At the northern end of Midford viaduct the site of the former Midford signalbox is now utilised as a car park for the Hope and Anchor Inn below. As well as the Somerset & Dorset this shot also clearly highlights the path of the GWR branch. Passenger traffic on this line ceased in 1925. Midford viaduct is an eight-arch structure of 168 yards length and marks the beginning of the double track section to Templecombe 32 miles to the south.

The carriages on the 9.03 am Bristol to Bournemouth West on Saturday 4 August 1962 are a mixture of a SR green three-coach set and LMS and BR maroon carriages. The train double headed by Nos 75072 and 73049 is approaching Midford A groundframe that controlled access to the goods yard. A solitary 13-ton mineral wagon is resident and although the presence of the crane lorry hints at other traffic I doubt it would have a greater capacity than the permanent 2-ton crane.

Zooming in towards Midford station site, it becomes clear why this location was chosen by the film makers to set the scene for *The Titfield Thunderbolt*. With a mainline, a branchline, canal, babbling brook and English country road all converging at a picturesque viaduct – not to mention the classic country pub – it must have been too good to miss! Even in 2012 the setting remains idyllic.

On the afternoon of Thursday 12 August 1965 Swindon-built '8F' 48444 and brake van pass the remains of Midford goods yard (where the rails had been lifted in June 1964) probably en route for Radstock and Norton Hill Colliery. The Midford down home was sited on the top of the 'Long Arch' (actually 37 yards long) and underneath it is a repeater arm for the wrong road signal sited on the station platform.

Midford station was of simple wooden construction. The single platform was cut into the hillside looking down on the picturesque valley below. The picture shows the former platform site to the right of the viaduct's end. Set on the hillside above is the stationmaster's house. As previously mentioned, the viaduct marks the beginning of the double track section to the south. Tales remain of single line tablets being surrendered to the roof of the Hope and Anchor public house which can be seen to the left of the line just before the B3110 road passes beneath the first arch of the viaduct!

Lower Twinhoe Underbridge

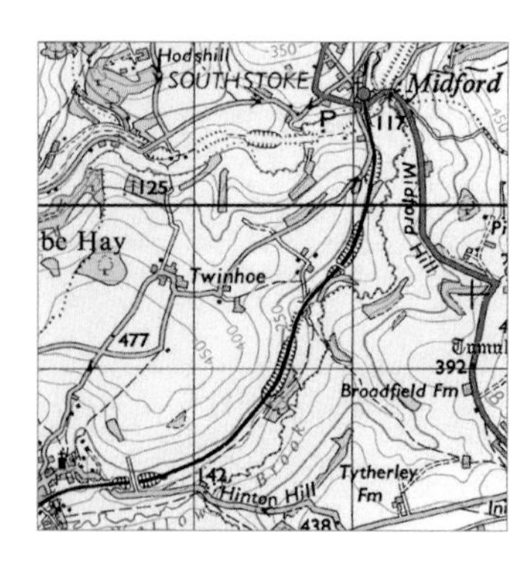

ABOVE This shot certainly lives up to the title 'Somerset & Dorset Line From Above'! Using the basic but effective aerial navigation technique of 'big to small' Peasedown St John can be identified as the central built up area in the middle distance with Radstock just visible to the far left. (Look closely and Wells mast can just be seen directly above on the far horizon!) Working towards the camera, Wellow is the closest built up area. From here the line can be traced back following the contours around the high ground and Hankley Woods until Twinhoe Bridge can be picked out at the bottom of the picture. Easy!

The line follows a twisting course as it swings through a series of reverse curves as a result of being engineered to follow the path of the old Somersetshire Coal Canal. Heading southeast it sweeps around the curve into Wellow. The village is seen in the centre of the picture with the built up area of Peasedown St John beyond. As we approach Wellow – only 6¾ miles from Bath – it is fascinating to ponder on the stunning scenery and architecture of the line so far. The number of photographs taken of trains sweeping around the reverse curves in the Midford valley reflects this and reaffirms the fondness in which this line is still held almost 50 years after the final train ran.

Wellow

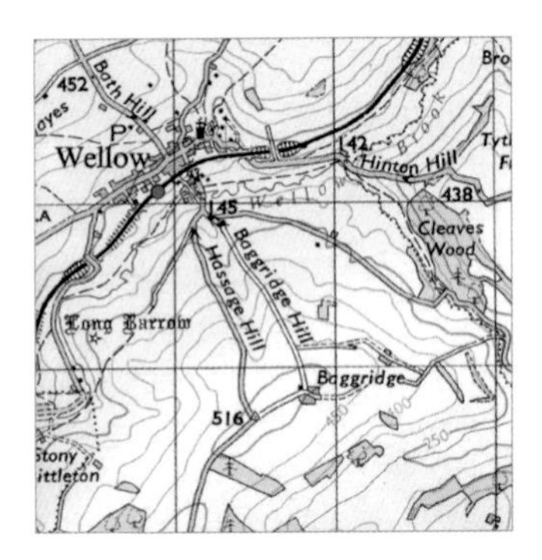

ABOVE The 14th century St Julian's church commands the skyline when seen from the trackbed approaching Wellow; from the air it isn't so prominent but still serves as a good reference feature. The line is now straddled by the Wellow Trekking Centre. This lies on the approach to the village and sits between the overbridge and the viaduct with the road running beneath. With difficult road access, the railway was well patronised and the station opened in 1874. It had a larger than average goods yard and benefitted from trade with a local forge producing agricultural machinery. The station itself was situated on the western side of the village next to the swimming pool visible on the far left of the photograph.

FACING PAGE This view presents the approach to Wellow in greater detail. The viaduct can be clearly identified with the Wellow Trekking Centre firmly established on the trackbed. The road passes under the viaduct and on towards the village in a series of s-bends. Taken from the northern side, this shot presents a good view of Wellow viaduct. This was another typically handsome Somerset & Dorset structure comprising of four arches and of 51 yards length.

Wellow Station and Signalbox

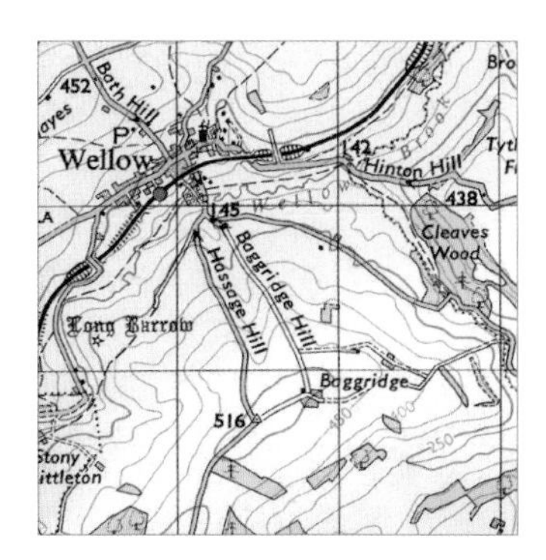

FACING PAGE An overhead view of Wellow looking towards the northeast. Using St Julian's church as a reference point, the line of the trackbed can be traced entering from the top of the picture before crossing the tennis court and running roughly parallel to the High Street. The station buildings can be seen just below the swimming pool in the centre of the picture! Wellow signalbox also survives but is harder to identify. Sited to the east of the station it can just be seen to the right of the rectangular brown roofed building set at right angles to the trackbed. The signalbox is nestling behind the centrally placed large green tree!

ABOVE With the line from Midford and Bath running in from the right this shot presents a fine view of the station area and buildings. It also highlights just how much local use has been made of the relatively flat trackbed; buildings, outbuildings and even swimming pools have appeared where the trains once ran. To the right of the shot – again using the rectangular building with blackened roof openings as a reference – the restored signalbox is visible to the right of the large green tree.

Templecombe engine No 75009 pulls away from Wellow station with the 3.20pm Bath to Templecombe stopping train on Saturday 2 June 1962. This train followed the down 'Pines Express' which left Bath at 3.9pm. The signal shows the SDJR practice of re-using two old rails for a post and a finial that may be a useful prototype for modellers!

Wellow station boasted both an up and a down platform. The main station buildings were constructed on the up platform. The area just above the row of parked cars was the former goods yard. As originally built the platform buildings comprised of a bay windowed stationmaster's office, a combined booking office and waiting room, and a ladies room. The down platform had a simple wooden shelter.

Foxcote

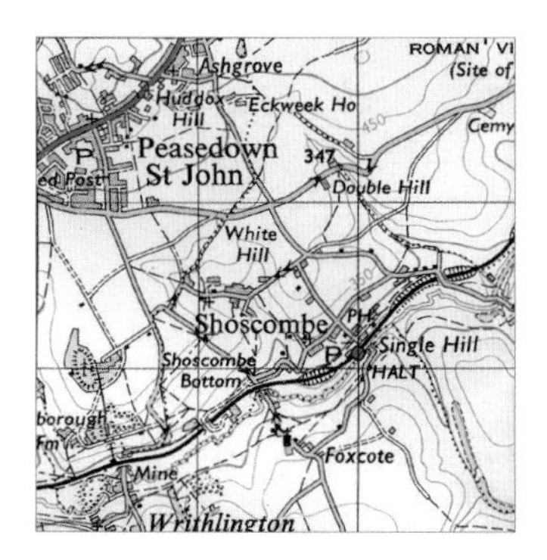

FACING PAGE Leaving Wellow the Somerset & Dorset continued to follow the line of the valley in a series of gentle reverse curves towards the southwest and the town of Radstock. The line taken by the railway can easily be traced from the air, contouring around features with descriptive names such as Double and Single Hill! Roughly midway between Wellow and Radstock the railway constructed Shoshcombe and Single Hill Halt in 1929. This was in response to the growing threat from local road competition. The halt was very basic – two Southern Railway style prefabricated concrete platforms – and no trace of it remains today. It was situated at the furthest end of the crescent shaped built up area seen in the upper section of this picture.

ABOVE In August 1876 the Somerset & Dorset suffered the worst accident in the line's history at Foxcote when two trains collided head on in what was then a single track section between Evercreech and Bath. Fifteen people died as an up relief special met a down working of supposedly empty coaching stock but which was subsequently found to be carrying workers returning to the Radstock area from a day out in Bath. The accident was attributed to poor working practice and bad communications. The crash site is roughly mid-point in this picture. To find it the roadway passing the four industrial units should be continued on in a straight line until it intersects with the trackbed. The nearest farm granary buildings further up the line on the right hand side were used as a temporary mortuary for the victims to aid in the identification process.

Duty 241 was the 7.00am Cleethorpes to Exmouth (SO) which normally only took a pilot if loaded to more than the eight coaches allowed for a '7F' between Bath and Evercreech Junction. On Saturday 3 September 1960 long term SDJR resident '2P' No 40564 pilots 53808 past the sidings for Writhlington Colliery on the approach to Radstock.

With the camera now positioned roughly over the Foxcote crash site this view indicates - even now - how difficult access to the area would have been. To add to the difficulties faced in the immediate aftermath of the crash, factor into this the darkness of a 19th century night in the country, dimly lit (or in this instance possibly unlit) oil signal lamps and the limitations of communication by signal telegraph only.

On a bright Saturday afternoon on 15 June 1963 75007 drifts past the entrance to Writhlington Colliery before stopping at Radstock. No 75007 had been transferred from Oxford to Templecombe in March 1963, hence the single chimney and small BR2 tender tender as opposed to the double chimney and BR1B tender of Nos 75071-3. This was the site of the infamous and illegal Foxcote signalbox at the heart of the fatal collision in 1876. It became a ground frame in 1877 and was removed when the line was doubled in 1894.

Radstock

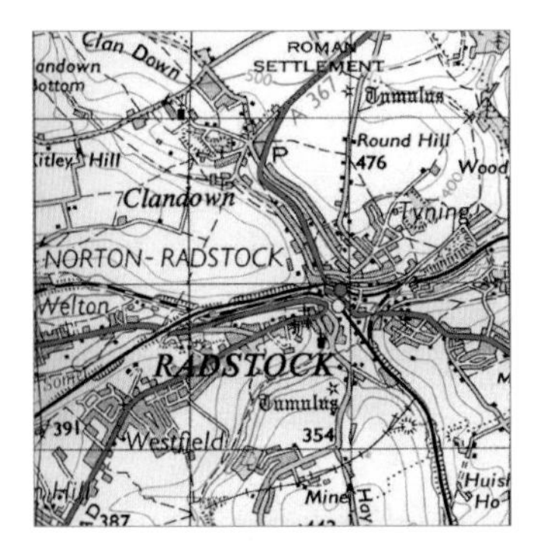

ABOVE Radstock is another example of a town on the Somerset & Dorset line where virtually all traces of the railway have been swept away, replaced by roads. A visitor to the area would find it difficult to imagine just how extensive the railway system once was in the town. Yet, from the air, some indications still remain. Radstock was the centre for the Somerset mining industry and was served by two stations – Radstock North (S&D) and Radstock West (GWR) – both of which were only a few yards apart. Looking from the south, the Somerset & Dorset entered from the east at a point just beyond the dense wooded area on the right of the picture. It passed through the northern part of the town, following the line of trees out to the left of the picture and crossing over the GWR's Bristol–Frome line by means of the five-arch viaduct visible towards the left of the treeline. The GWR line entered from the bottom of the shot and curved around the right hand side of the present Co-operative superstore (visible in the centre of town) before running parallel to the Somerset & Dorset as far as the five-arch viaduct.

No 76015 slowly draws into Radstock station with the 1.10pm Bath to Bournemouth on 3 February 1965 under the ringed calling-on arm showing that the level crossing gates are still closed across the railway. In the background the safety valves on 'Jinty' 47544 have lifted on shed prior to its following the passenger service up the line to Midsomer Norton to shunt Norton Hill Colliery.

No 48444 eases empty wagons for Norton Hill Colliery past the disused Radstock East or Radstock North A signalbox on 3 February 1965. The waste heaps from Ludlows and Tyning Collieries dominate the skyline. To the right can be seen the abutments of the bridge that took the tubline from Tynings Colliery over the SDJR until it was demolished in 1960. This bridge was the reason for the elevation of the signalbox which was constructed in 1894 when the section from Wellow to Radstock was doubled.

In the last year of service of the '2Ps' on the SDJR, 40700 and 34041 *Wilton* drift down the 1 in 50 and pass over the North Somerset line of the Great Western on Saturday 15 July 1961. This is probably the Bournemouth to Liverpool train as 34041 worked back to its home shed Bournemouth on the 10.55 Manchester Piccadilly to Bournemouth West train

Using a closer viewpoint it is possible to begin tracing the site of the former Radstock North station. Working from the large superstore in the centre of town, the multiple road junction to the right hand side marks the route of the busy A367 which crosses the trackbed of both railways before running out towards the top of the picture. The white minibus is approaching the site of the GWR's level crossing and that company's station sat in the present day treeline just below the vehicle. Continuing further right, a larger crescent shaped set of trees hides the recreation area where Radstock North once stood. With two level crossings so close together it was inevitable that road traffic suffered heavy delays. Although today's picture may indicate otherwise, the reality is that traffic on the A367 is still slow moving through this area – despite the railway's disappearance!

This view repositions the camera to the northern side of Radstock. Just beside the crescent shaped set of trees in the left of the picture a recreation area can be seen. A memorial to the mining industry in the shape of a colliery winding wheel is set just off the A367 road. This marks the site of Radstock North station. Continuing left along the former trackbed the line curves gently away until it passes in front of the large area of trees visible towards the edge of the photograph. Housing has been built on this land which once encompassed both the goods yard and a twin road stone-built engine shed. Virtually every freight train heading south required banking over the $7\frac{1}{2}$ miles to Masbury summit. Once again, it is striking from this view how little of the town's railway heritage remains evident. From leaving the down platform and crossing the A367, southbound trains began the climb into the Mendips. At this point the Somerset & Dorset line ran in parallel with GWR metals out to the west. This area today has been redeveloped with part of it containing the children's play park seen at the bottom of the picture.

Five Arches – Midsomer Norton Station

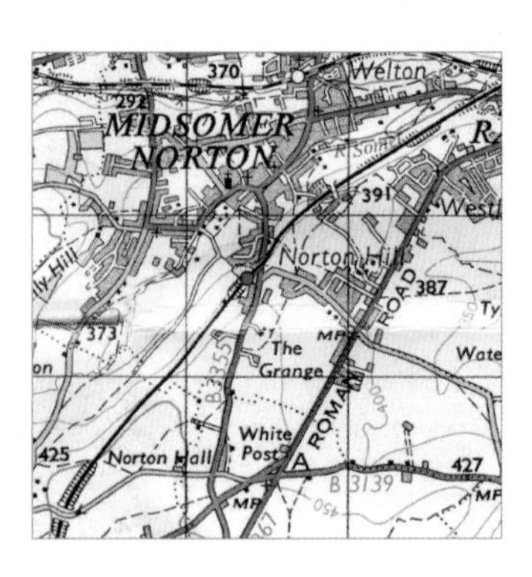

ABOVE Leaving Radstock the railway ran out to the west, its path hidden by the trees along the centre section of this photograph. It climbed steeply on a gradient of 1 in 55 which enabled it to turn south and cross over the GWR line before continuing towards Midsomer Norton. The viaduct, centred in the picture, was officially the North Somerset viaduct but was known locally as the 'Five Arches'. A further bridge crossed over the A362 Somervale Road at the far right of the shot. This was demolished in 1982.

FACING PAGE This picture show the Five Arches in greater detail. The trackbed is accessible and closer examination of the scene will reveal someone taking advantage of this – and the absence of trains – to enjoy a picnic in peaceful isolation!

The camera has now been repositioned high over Midsomer Norton. The railway follows the treeline from the bottom of the picture and stretches away to the southwest. From height, there is little indication of the climb faced by southbound trains although the line of hills in the distance gives some clue. In the centre of the photograph Midsomer Norton station can just be distinguished. The rake of preserved rolling stock stabled at the site belonging to the Somerset & Dorset Railway Heritage Trust sits just beyond the B3355 as it intersects the line. Much further left, the A367 hints at its Roman origins as it runs straight towards the southwest. Between these two roads the cleared area towards the left of the picture marks the position of the former Norton Hill Colliery. Access to these workings was gained via the Somerset & Dorset line just north of Midsomer Norton station. In the distance, the line continues uphill towards Chilcompton and beyond.

Midsomer Norton Station

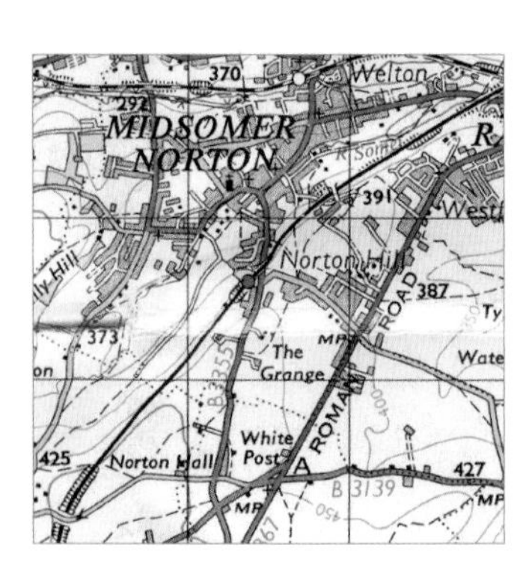

ABOVE Midsomer Norton station occupies the site towards the centre of the photograph. Twelve miles out from Bath Road Junction, southbound trains have already been climbing steeply for $1\frac{3}{4}$ miles since leaving Radstock. The gradient of 1 in 50 eases through the station limits to 1 in 300, only to quickly resume at 1 in 53. From the air this is not readily apparent, but from the footplate of one of the line's iconic '7Fs', labouring uphill, the climb would seem relentless! The amount of newly built housing on both sides of the line is noteworthy in this shot.

FACING PAGE Opened as Midsomer Norton station in 1874, the name was changed on several occasions, becoming Midsomer Norton and Welton, then Midsomer Norton Upper and finally Midsomer Norton South. In common with many stations at the time, great pride was taken in presentation and appearance; Midsomer Norton excelled in this respect and was renowned for its floral displays. The station was a consistent winner of the 'Best Kept Station' award from 1953 to 60 and the greenhouse maintained on the up platform was a well-known feature. This has been faithfully recreated and can be seen next to the restored signalbox. Closer inspection of this photograph will reveal just how much work has been done by volunteers to restore the station to its former glory – no mean feat since the trackbed was infilled after closure. The site is well worth a visit if the reader is in the area. The running line is slowly being extended and in this view a two-car DMU sits in the down platform.

No 53807 glides into Midsomer Norton just before 4pm with the 1.10pm Bournemouth to Bath on Saturday 1 September 1962. The horticultural efforts of the staff are evident everywhere in hanging baskets, tubs and beds. If the passenger with the dog is travelling, he should have two tickets!

'2P' No 40634 and '7F' 53803 work back south through Midsomer Norton station light engine on Saturday 15 July 1961 having worked north earlier in the day. The single lamp at the top of the smokebox was the SDJR code for light engine workings.

No 53807 leaves Midsomer Norton on the 1.10pm Bournemouth to Bath on Saturday 1 September 1962 past the immaculately tended garden. Midsomer Norton was possibly unique in having a greenhouse alongside its signalbox! On the right can be seen the height restriction of 10ft 9in (3.3m) on the bridge over Silver Street. The road was so steep that although this was the clearance on the uphill side, on the downhill side it was nearer 13ft (4m) and hence the danger for large loads coming uphill and the reason for its speedy demolition after the lifting of the rails, to the chagrin of the Somerset & Dorset Railway Heritage Trust who now occupy the station site.

Such is the enduring popularity of the Somerset & Dorset line that, at first glance, this shot could be mistaken for another model railway layout depicting times gone by. It is, however, the real Midsomer Norton station as photographed in 2012. As the working centre of the Somerset & Dorset Railway Heritage Trust it clearly illustrates the work achieved to date in restoring the station and its surroundings to their former glory. The track layout is well represented and the small two-road goods yard, one of which passes through the stone built goods shed, stands out at the bottom of the picture. A Class 08 diesel shunter sits in the headshunt whilst a road/rail vehicle occupies the up line just beyond the trailing crossover. Despite the best efforts of preservationists there are some limitations to expansion that will prove difficult to overcome. This view clearly shows the northern limit imposed by the removal of Silver Street Bridge over the B3355. Deemed too low to allow modern lorries and buses to pass safely underneath, it was dismantled and the area landscaped. This presents a physical barrier to any further drive aimed at restoring sections of the line north towards Radstock.

This panoramic view encompasses the climb out of Radstock, just visible at the top right of the picture, and the path of the trackbed as it passes Midsomer Norton on the left of the shot. The station is situated at the top of a hill to the south of its namesake town. Comparison of earlier OS maps and the current landscape will show just how much the town has grown and how it now borders on former railway land. Midsomer Norton expanded rapidly during the railway's lifetime; industries within the town included paper, footwear and timber building manufacture. The former site of Norton Hill Colliery stands out clearly as the cleared area to the right and beyond the station site. The line continues towards the bottom (southwest) of the picture as it climbs towards Chilcompton Tunnel.

'Jinty' No 47465 is shunted into the station sidings at Midsomer Norton on a rather murky Monday 1 April 1963 in between shunting Norton Hill Colliery sidings. The van immediately behind the engine looks like a gunpowder van and the schoolboy is showing an unhealthy interest!

The classic SDJR combination of '2P' 4-4-0 No 40563 and Armstrong Whitworth built '4F' 0-6-0 No 44561 slog through Midsomer Norton station with the 7.00am Cleethorpes to Exmouth SO on 15 July 1961. At Templecombe an Exmouth Junction engine would take over for the run to Sidmouth Junction hence the '4F' would not be called upon to do more than manage the train on its own between Evercreech Junction and Templecombe.

Chilcompton Tunnel

ABOVE The camera now looks out to the east over Chilcompton Tunnel. The tunnel itself – 66 yards long – is marked by the long, light green field with the cattle grazing just off to one side. Today the landscape is dramatically different from Somerset & Dorset days. The approach to the tunnel from the north was previously made through a steep sided cutting, over 40ft deep and stretching for $^1/_2$ mile. The cutting has since disappeared; infill from industrial waste topped with topsoil has returned the land to meadow. The southern tunnel portals can just be distinguished by the single-track road which passes just to the right side of the shot.

FACING PAGE This is another view of the northern section of Chilcompton Tunnel. Once a favoured location to photograph trains from the north as they laboured uphill through the deep cutting towards the narrow tunnel entrance, now only those actively seeking to trace the railway's path would be aware of where it once passed. An aerial perspective is invaluable; anyone passing on the narrow road would have no indication whatsoever.

One of the famous locations on the Bath Extension is this view from the hill above the Chilcompton Tunnels looking back towards Midsomer Norton. Here the 7.43am Bradford to Bournemouth SO is headed by '9F' No 92001 on Saturday 1 September 1962. The fireman clearly has everything under control as the safety valves are showing a feather but maybe an injector is giving trouble.

The southern portals of Chilcompton Tunnel can still be seen. An access track has been cut from the roadway above allowing use of the tunnel entrance as an agricultural store. The portals themselves have been kept clear of vegetation. The twin tunnel bores are a reminder that the line was originally built as single track and subsequently doubled as traffic demanded.

Chilcompton Station

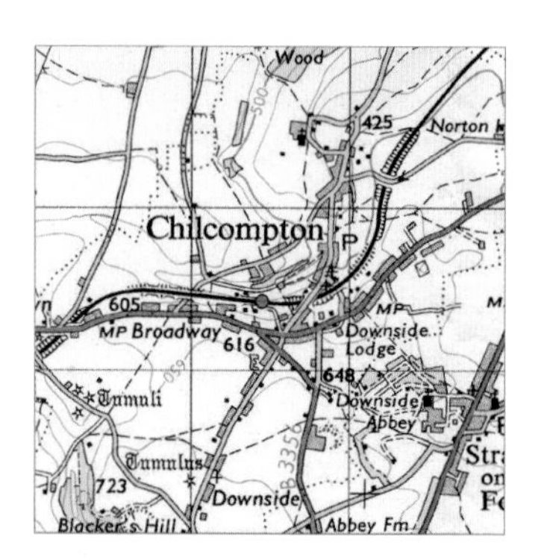

ABOVE Chilcompton station is reached 14 miles after leaving Bath Road Junction. The summit of the climb at Masbury is still some 3½ miles distant but, as at Midsomer Norton, the gradient eases to 1 in 300 through the station itself. Looking from the southeast and once again using treelines to track the railway's path, the southern portals of Chilcompton Tunnel can be seen in the right hand side of the picture. The line then sweeps across this view in a right hand curve as it approaches Chilcompton. There is now nothing left of the station itself, formerly located on the far left mid-point of the picture between the housing estate and the treeline. The only readily identifiable piece of railway infrastructure is Bridge 51, roughly in the centre of the shot. The B3139 Wells Road runs along the bottom of the picture.

FACING PAGE Repositioning the camera to the north of the approach to Chilcompton Bridge 51 disappears in the treeline although the sweep of the trackbed is still apparent. The station site is marked by the line of darker green trees at the top of the picture. Chilcompton had two staggered platforms but no footbridge. It provided an oasis for banking engines on their return to Radstock and therefore had a large water tower situated on the southern side of the station. A siding on the down side was also provided to accommodate road deliveries of coal from New Rock Colliery which was then transferred to rail for onward shipment.

No 53809 is the pilot from Evercreech Junction to Bath for No 34103 *Calstock* on the 12.20pm SO Bournemouth West to Nottingham on 1 September 1962 as the train rolls downhill past Chilcompton signalbox on the 1 in 50 ruling gradient. The Vauxhall, presumably belonging to the signalman, is parked in front of the crane and goods shed and a pile of domestic coal. No 53809 is happily still with us and based at Butterley.

No 92220 *Evening Star* was re-allocated to Bath to work the last 'Pines Express' in August and September 1962 but returned in August 1963 in response to a request by Bath MPD for loan of two Class 5 4-6-0s to cover a temporary shortage. Nos 92224 and 92220 were transferred and proved rather an embarrassment as coal consumption was excessive on three- or four-coach trains and the engines were too long to be turned on the turntables at Evercreech Junction or Templecombe. Here 92220 approaches Moorewood from Chilcompton with the 4.21pm semi-fast from Bath to Bournemouth on Saturday 14 September 1963.

Taken from the north, this is another view of Bridge 51. Once again, the spread of modern housing can be noted although one of the roads in the upper right area of the picture pays homage to the past with the name of 'Pines Close'. As with many of today's pictures, it is still possible to identify specific older buildings that can be cross-referenced to previous photographic studies of the line. The square detached house (just short of the treeline on the right side of the picture) can be seen in a 1960 photograph published in Mac Hawkins' *The Somerset & Dorset Then and Now* – a fascinating and time consuming form of archaeological detective work! Visual airborne navigation is a skill still taught to pilots – especially military pilots – using clear landmarks including railways and prominent former railway features which stand out from the air. Also standing out to this military pilot is the Redan Inn, marked on earlier OS maps and still visible from the air at the crossroads towards the bottom of the picture!

Chilcompton station occupied the area in the centre of this photograph, running along the treeline to the right of the square green field. The western station limits are now in use as part of a trailer storage site. The station was also used at the beginning and end of school term time as a destination for special trains conveying pupils to the nearby Downside School. Looking out to the west, the line continued climbing towards the summit just north of Binegar. This is located just beyond the quarry workings in the upper left of the picture. Southbound engine crews considered the worst of the climb to be over once the railway crossed under the B3139 road. This point can be seen by tracing the road running parallel to the trackbed beyond Chilcompton and then noting where they intersect as the line turns south. Those with eagle eyes will just be able to identify Wells Mast on the skyline in the distance

Binegar Station Site

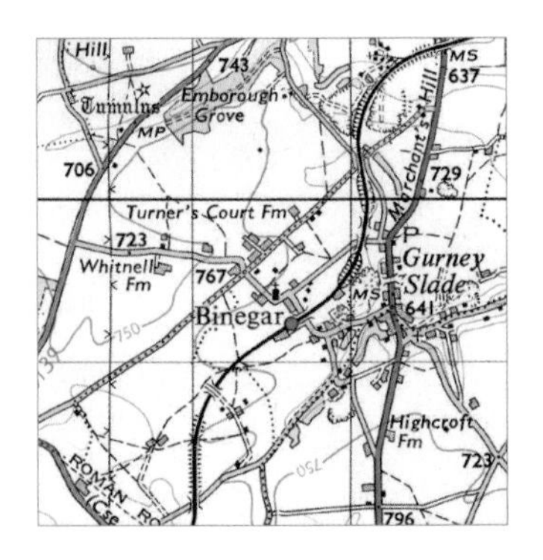

ABOVE The stone quarry in this picture provides a link, having been visible from the previous location at Chilcompton. Looking to the northeast the built up area around Midsomer Norton and Radstock can still be seen. The line, by now only a mile short of the summit, continues its climb through the Mendips. It passes down the side of the curved wood in the centre of the shot before reaching Binegar station, the site of which is in the bottom left corner of this view. Down freight trains were banked to the summit at Masbury, the banker then being uncoupled and returning 'wrong road' to Binegar en route to Radstock for their next duty. As a further treat for those comparing today's aerial view to OS maps of yesteryear, there is at least one long-standing public house prominent in this view! (The Horse and Jockey located at the opposite apex of the field to the right of the station site.)

FACING PAGE The camera has now been repositioned virtually overhead Binegar station site. The former trackbed runs from the top to the bottom of the picture, initially following the curving treeline mentioned in the panoramic view. Binegar church can be seen on the far left of the shot. The platforms and station buildings have been demolished, their place taken by the domestic housing built along the line's path. However, the station cottages and the long, stone built goods shed have survived and can be seen at the bottom of the picture.

Nos 40563 and 53810 make their way as light engines from Bath back to Templecombe on the afternoon of Saturday 29 July 1961. In the background can be seen the Portway Bridge and the Moorewood Sidings up starter, the down home being obscured by the smoke from the engines. The sidings in the foreground were installed to take coal from Moorewood Colliery but when this traffic ceased in the 1930s the sidings thereafter were used for wagon storage.

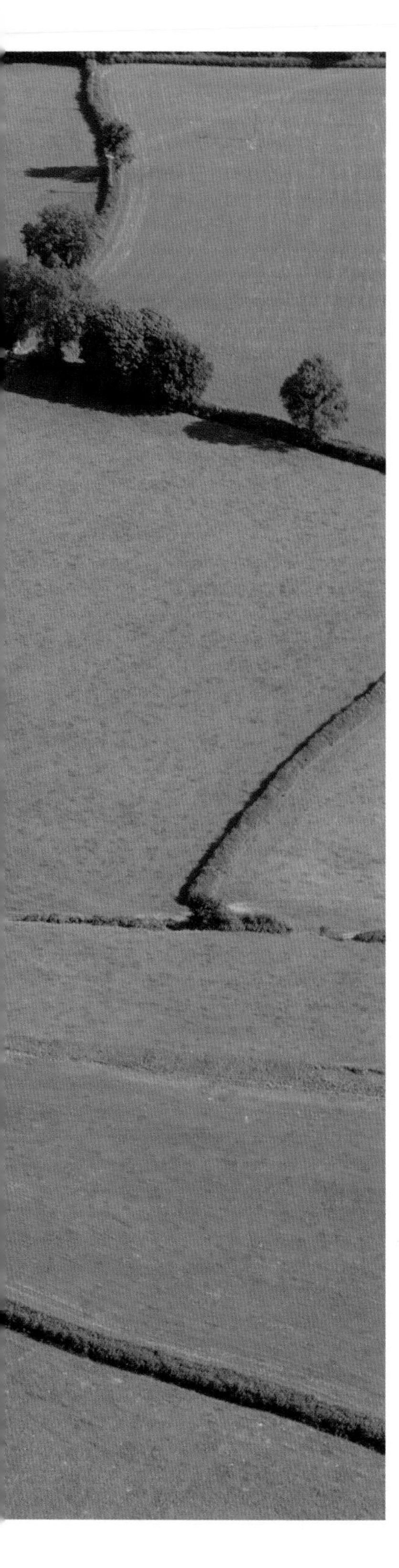

Afternoon sunshine on Saturday 4 March 1961 illuminates No 40563 as it draws into Binegar station past Stationmaster Norman Down with a stopping train from Bath, believed to be the 3.20pm to Templecombe. The vans visible in the background on the Mendip Stone sidings are probably stored wagons.

The long stone building centred in this view sat to the south of Binegar station. It was originally constructed as the terminus of a narrow gauge light railway. This belonged to the Oakhill Brewery and was built in 1904 for transporting its products from the brewery itself for onward shipment. The brewery line was closed in 1921 and the stone building was converted for use as a standard gauge goods shed. It found use as a local coal merchant's store after the line closed but, as can be seen, has since been restored and redeveloped. The two stone cottages immediately to the left are the only other surviving railway buildings, having been used as the stationmaster and signalman's residences. The platforms and trackbed ran through the site of the new housing estate on the left of the picture, appropriately called 'The Beechings' by its first owner! A second residential building is nearing completion on the site of the station's former platforms. Binegar station was temporarily renamed 'Boiland' and starred in the British Railways instructional film on single line working.

Masbury Summit and Station

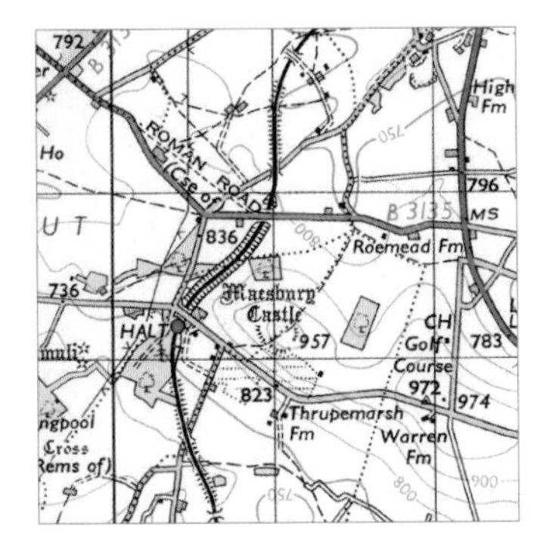

FACING PAGE The summit of the line was reached just beyond milepost $17\frac{1}{2}$ at a height of 811 feet above sea level. At this point the gradient for southbound trains changed from 1 in 63 up to 1 in 50 down as the descent towards Evercreech Junction began. The summit was sited in a deep cutting between Nine Acre Wood and Furze Wood, the square wood seen on the left of this picture. The cutting has since been partly infilled and is now wooded itself. As a favourite photographic location of the renowned Ivo Peters, it was at this spot that his ashes were scattered after his death in 1989. The site of Masbury station (halt) is concealed in the wooded area in the centre of the photograph.

ABOVE The previously mentioned Furze Wood just appears at the left hand edge of the picture as the line now descends, curving left to pass through Masbury station which is concealed by the trees to the right of the road. Prominent in this picture is the Iron Age hill fort, Maesbury Castle, from which the station derives its name. Shepton Mallet is just visible as the built up area in the upper right section of the shot.

The 11.00am Bath to Evercreech Junction goods loaded to 25 wagons on Tuesday 11 February 1964 so No 48468 was banked by 47506 from Radstock to the summit of the line at Masbury. No 47506 will have picked up the banking staff at Binegar allowing it to return 'wrong line', having seen the train safely over the summit.

FACING PAGE Southbound trains, having crested the summit just beyond the right boundary of this view, now descend at 1 in 50 to pass through Masbury station. The station is now a private residence and the former stationmaster's house stands prominent in the centre of this scene. All the main station buildings were constructed on the up platform. The stationmaster's house was noteworthy for its large bay window and the gothic stone carving above. Sandwiched between this and the booking office/waiting room was a signalbox. This has now been replaced by an extension to the living quarters. Whilst trains from Bath now enjoyed a respite after the gruelling climb from Radstock, it should be noted that up trains calling at the station faced a difficult restart on the 1 in 50 gradient! Once again, trees have grown unchecked and drivers passing along the road crossing over the line on Bridge 70 might find it difficult to sight the station through the vegetation. Without prior knowledge they would probably never guess at its former existence from just a fleeting glimpse.

ABOVE As the camera is positioned overhead more details of the remaining station buildings emerge. Opened in 1874 this was the highest station in the Mendips but suffered from serving a scattered rural community. It was subsequently reduced to halt status in 1935 and became unstaffed in 1938. There was a brief resurgence in traffic during World War 2, helped by the proximity of a nearby US Army camp. During this time steps were added from the roadway to the down platform. As can be seen from the photograph, some infilling of the trackbed has been carried out and the area given over to domestic activities!

The 3.20pm Bath to Templecombe train on Saturday 14 September 1963 is hauled by No 44422 and has just come over the summit and drops down towards the road bridge at Masbury. It will only be stopping at Masbury Halt if notice has been given to the guard. The elevation here (just under 1,000ft above sea level) is evident as the leaves have already started to turn.

The fireman has done the hard work with only another half mile to go to the summit as No 53806 pounds through Masbury with the 10.40am Exmouth to Cleethorpes SO train on Saturday 29 July 1961. The train this day loaded to nine coaches and comprised two Southern four-coach sets with a strengthening coach between. No doubt somebody at Exeter was hoping that their stock would be coming back next week!

The southern end of Masbury station site is now at the bottom of the picture as we look down towards the south and the continuing descent towards Shepton Mallet via Winsor Hill Tunnel. Note the prominent blue garden nursery building which will prove useful for orientation in the next series of pictures.

Winsor Hill Tunnel

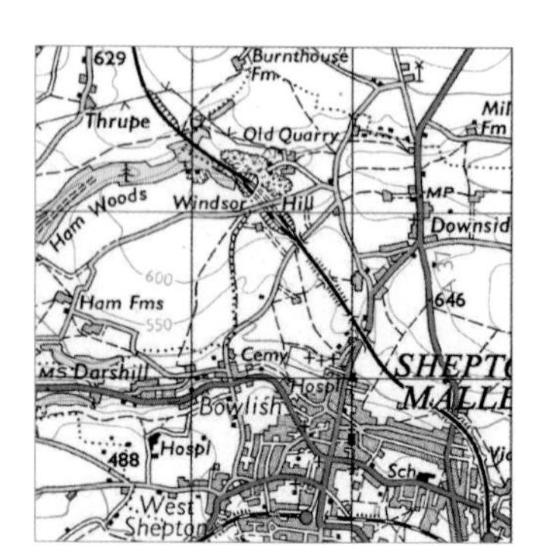

ABOVE Chew Valley Lake is visible in the distance as we look back towards the north. The prominent blue structures mentioned in the final picture of Masbury station can be seen midpoint in the upper third section of this photograph allowing the path of the line to be traced as it continues its descent towards Winsor Hill and Ham Wood at the bottom of the picture. It should be noted that many older maps – and previous line histories – use the alternative to the modern spelling of Windsor. In keeping with this convention Winsor will be used here too. The twin bores of Winsor Hill Tunnel are situated just to the south of this panoramic shot, lying $19\frac{1}{2}$ miles from Bath Road Junction and still on a falling gradient of 1 in 50 for southbound trains.

FACING PAGE The camera is now looking northwest. In the far distance the city of Wells can just be distinguished to the left hand side of the picture. Wells Mast sits in the centre of the skyline and Chew Valley Lake edges into view on the right. Ham Wood now occupies the centre of the shot with Winsor Hill Farm to the right and Rosamund Green Farm to the left. The road bisecting the two farms is Ham Lane and the tunnel passes beneath it with the northern portals just beyond the road line, the southern portals below it and roughly level with the farm complex. Infilling to the south and tree growth to the north now make it extremely difficult to identify these railway features from the air.

Bath Standard Class 4 No 75073 bursts out of Winsor Hill Tunnel on the afternoon of Saturday 4 August 1962 with a Bath to Templecombe local train. This was the original bore, a new bore being dug to the west of this for the second line in the 1880s.

Such was the extent of stone quarrying in the Mendips that no less than three quarries existed in the vicinity of Winsor Hill: Ham Wood Quarry on the up side of the line with Winsor Hill and Downside Quarries on the down side. All three closed before the Somerset & Dorset. A stone built signalbox constructed between the two running lines to the north of the tunnel controlled access to the quarry sidings. Of course, no sign of this structure remains today. Although Ham Lane can be clearly seen running through the centre of the picture, the exact location of the tunnel cannot be visually determined from height.

Winsor Hill Tunnel consisted of twin bores, the down line 239 yards long as originally built and the up line shorter at 126 yards long. By slewing the up line slightly when doubling the formation in 1892 the contractor was able to shorten the tunnel length, thereby saving costs. The tunnel site is now in the bottom left corner of the picture as the line continues southeast towards the market town of Shepton Mallet. The roadway between Rosamund Green Farm (Forum Lane) was crossed by Bridge 78 - demolished in the early 1990s. Those familiar with the area will be able to pinpoint Bath Road Viaduct and Charlton Viaduct to the left of Shepton Mallet. If not, the next set of pictures will help.

Bath Road Viaduct

ABOVE Moving closer to Shepton Mallet, the Somerset & Dorset line can be seen continuing downhill from Winsor Hill Tunnel (just off the bottom left corner of the picture) and approaching the built up area from the northwest. The line skirts the eastern side of the town, curving to the south as it does so. Bath Road Viaduct still stands; it spans the B3136 Bath Road 1½ miles south of the tunnel. Once again, the railway's path is highlighted by trees. Following it towards the edge of own the viaduct can just be picked out in this picture.

FACING PAGE TOP This is a closer view of the viaduct with Bath Road passing beneath towards Shepton Mallet off to the right. The structure is 118 yards long and carries the railway over the road on six spans. One advantage of an aerial perch is that it is often possible to see the potential for a collision on the road far in advance of the motorist concerned; the driver of the car travelling towards the viaduct and Shepton will have to hope the cars approaching from the opposite direction regain their correct lane soon!

FACING PAGE BOTTOM As built the viaduct was, of course, single line. During the line's doubling in 1892 the up side was widened. This is the side closest to the camera in this shot. Unfortunately this side of the viaduct suffered a collapse during a winter storm early in 1946. Six months of enforced single line working was necessary before it was rebuilt later that year.

FACING PAGE Although smaller than the other remaining railway viaduct in Shepton Mallet, this one is still an imposing structure within its immediate surroundings. It towers over Bath Road with the path of the former trackbed clearly visible to the north in this overhead view.

ABOVE Taken from the northeast, here is one final view of Bath Road Viaduct. The next series of pictures depicting the path of the line through Shepton Mallet and beyond will illustrate just how much of the railway's former infrastructure has been swept aside over the years since closure. Had the line been saved and faced a resurgence in the style of the Settle & Carlisle route, one can only imagine the sights and sounds that the owner of the large detached house to the north of the viaduct would have been able to enjoy!

Charlton Viaduct and Shepton Mallet

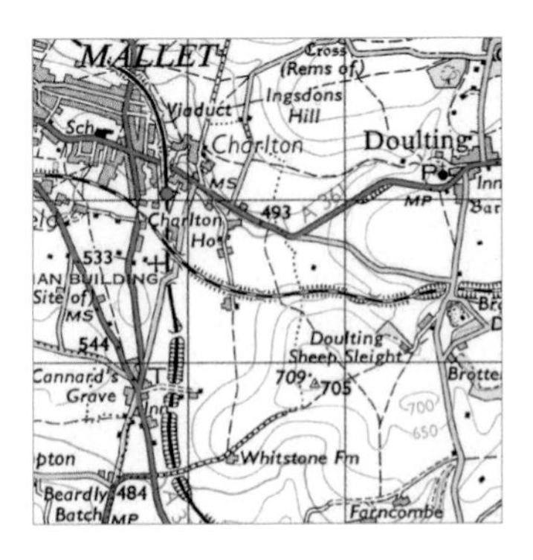

ABOVE Those fortunate enough to have flown over all or part of the former Somerset & Dorset will appreciate that certain features are visible from some distance – weather permitting of course! Such is the case with Wells Mast. Towns also stand out and this is the case here. The railway skirts the eastern edge of Shepton Mallet, carried on the striking Charlton Viaduct. Those who have tracked the railway's path through previous photographs will be able to follow the line back towards the Mendips in this shot.

FACING PAGE Charlton Viaduct remains instantly recognisable as a major part of the line's infrastructure. At 317 yards long it is still largely intact and has even had its surface tarmacked since tracks were lifted. At the bottom left of the picture the approach to Charlton Road station is now overgrown. Today's road traveller on the busy A37 sees nothing of this sight; the road passes along the top of the picture and the view is obscured. Indeed, the motorist is far more likely to be distracted by the former Babycham production plant – complete, for a while, with a roof mounted reindeer advertising the product!

No 44558 was photographed earlier at Gurney Slade and traffic on the A37, on Tuesday 8 December 1964, allowed a rapid transit to take this picture of the 11.00am Bath to Evercreech Junction goods as it passed Shepton Mallet.

Here is a further panoramic view as the camera is repositioned to the western side of Shepton Mallet. The railway can be seen passing over Bath Road Viaduct on the left before sweeping around the town's outer limits to cross the A37 just before Charlton Viaduct, visible in the centre of the scene.

Although not immediately apparent from this angle, Bath Road Viaduct is hidden by the treeline on the bottom right of the picture. What can be easily seen is the graceful right hand curve of Charlton Road Viaduct just beyond the A37 main road running through the centre of Shepton Mallet. The station, which was known as Charlton Road, no longer exists. In its place is the extensive industrial estate on the eastern edge of the town. Looking south once more, another prominent treeline crossing from left to right marks the passage of the former GWR branch line from Witham to Yatton – part of which is preserved and operated as the East Somerset Railway further out to the east. This branch line crossed over the Somerset & Dorset south of Charlton Road station.

ABOVE Whitstone School and the Shepton Mallet Leisure Centre sit to the right hand side of this view. The brewery complex fills the centre of the picture with the A37 crossing from left to right. Charlton Road Viaduct can now be seen from its western side. Trains crossing the viaduct experienced several gradient changes. Up trains departing Shepton Mallet for the north enjoyed a brief downhill section at 1 in 55 which changed once on the viaduct such that they left the structure climbing at 1 in 55. This ensured that departing traffic enjoyed the benefit of a favourable start before beginning the climb towards the Mendips' summit some 3½ miles to the north.

FACING PAGE This view of Charlton viaduct indicates how much restoration work has been undertaken since the structure passed from BR ownership. Showerings, former owners of the brewery complex, not only undertook this work but also maintained the gardens and Mill Pond Lake seen to the right of the view. The viaduct is 67 feet high, carrying the trackbed for 317 yards over 27 arches. A feature of the construction is that the ninth and eighteenth arches are thicker than the others, whilst every third arch is additionally buttressed on the outside (down side) to guard against lateral forces from trains. Charlton Road (A361) is crossed just beyond the row of trees. From this point on there remains no trace of the station approach or of Charlton Road station itself.

On the Saturday after Easter 28 April 1962 the down 'Pines Express' crosses Charlton Road viaduct and the Shepton Mallet up starter (tall enough to be sighted over the footbridge on which the photographer is standing) with Templecombe Standard Class 4 75023 piloting Standard Class 5 73052 between Bath and Evercreech. The sidings on the right were the province of the Signal and Telegraph Department, hence the interesting rolling stock.

Motorists leaving Shepton Mallet on the A37 towards Bath might catch an occasional glimpse of the embankment leading to the viaduct as they ascend the hill to the right of the photograph. That quick glimpse might cause the unwary to assume that the stone building immediately beside the line was the town's former station. It was, in fact, a school – now serving as a factory clearance shop for a well-known clothing firm. But ... what a location for a school!

Charlton Road Station Site

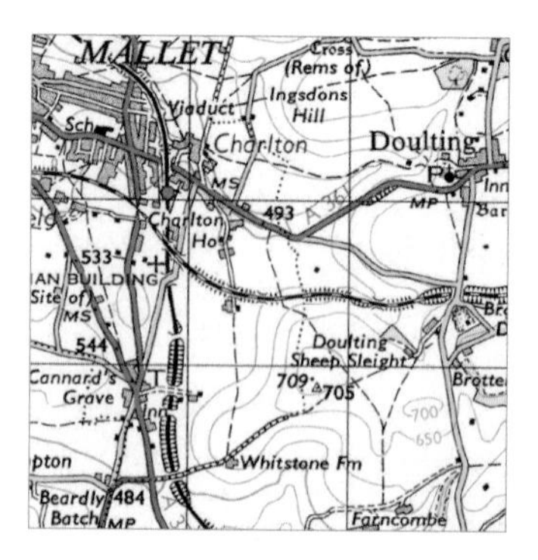

ABOVE This picture illustrates how the Somerset & Dorset's station was built on the edge of the town. Opened in 1874, the station was renamed Shepton Mallet (Charlton Road) in 1949. The GWR line, seen entering from the left, disappears towards the centre of Shepton Mallet where its station, High Street, enjoyed a more central location.

FACING PAGE Looking from the south, the point at which the line crossed GWR metals for the fourth time since leaving Bath can be seen just short of the square green industrial unit. The original stone bridge carrying the GWR line overhead was supplemented with a steel span extension when the up line was doubled in 1892.

The infamous occasion on Saturday 11 August 1962 is recorded when No 34043 *Combe Martin* had worked a relief up from Bournemouth to Bath and was booked to return light engine. On a busy Saturday there were few paths so at driver Donald Beale's suggestion they returned coupled ahead of 92245 on the 7.40am Bradford to Bournemouth West SO, here seen passing Shepton Mallet.

After a little over 21¼ miles from Bath Road Junction southbound trains arrived at Shepton Mallet (Charlton Road) station. The station had an extensive layout with sidings provided for quarry traffic, a local lime works and the normal goods requirements of a thriving market town. The line's signals department was also based here until 1930. Looking at this picture, nothing from that period has survived. Following on from the line of trees leading off the viaduct the station ran across the site now occupied by the industrial estate. The line crossed beneath the GWR's branch just beyond the parked orange trailer units seen in the left of the picture. The station had a larger than average water tank situated on the down side. After the strenuous climb over the Mendip Hills virtually all down freights stopped here to replenish water. Once underway again they faced a short climb – gentle by Somerset & Dorset standards at 1 in 70 – before beginning the final descent to Evercreech at 1 in 50. This descent commenced in Cannards Grave Cutting. Like the station, this cutting has also disappeared. Notorious for blockages caused by drifting snow in winter, it was filled in, dressed with topsoil and returned to farming use.

Prestleigh Viaduct

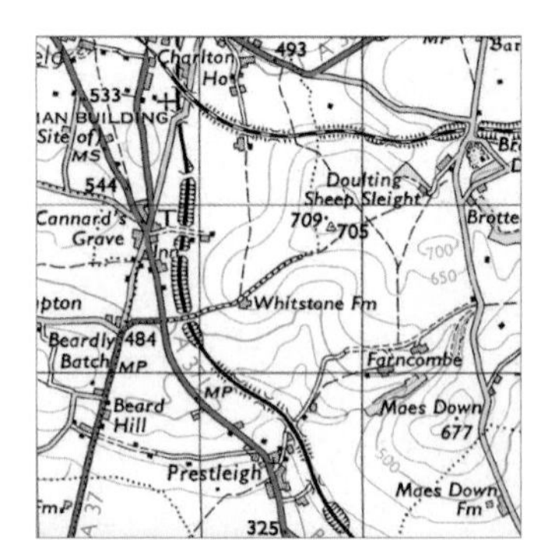

ABOVE Prestleigh Viaduct, another graceful stone structure, consisted of 11 spans and sat roughly halfway between Shepton Mallet and Evercreech. It was demolished in January 1993 having been assessed as structurally unsound as a result of years of neglect following the line's closure. Looking to the north in this view, Shepton Mallet can be seen in the middle distance. The Royal Bath and West of England Showground occupies the lower half of the picture with the A371 passing down the eastern side. At the north eastern corner lies the village of Prestleigh. The group of trees to the right of the village marks the site of the former viaduct. The disused trackbed can be traced running south from here towards Evercreech New station. To the north, all traces of the line have disappeared; as previously described, Cannards Grave Cutting to the south of Shepton Mallet has been infilled and the formation returned to farmland. Only by very careful inspection and comparison with OS mapping can the line's path be determined. It tracks around the left side of Whitstone Hill – roughly paralleling the road – until reaching the outskirts of Shepton. It then crosses the site of the large industrial unit prominent on the town's southern edge. As a further clue for the eagle-eyed, a grey farm storage building sits on the trackbed between the viaduct and the town.

Without the detailed explanation accompanying the panoramic shot this would simply appear to be a random picture of a small village and some trees! The viaduct spanned the minor road leading from the village, gently curving between the two groups of trees which now dominate the trackbed. To the north, little trace of the railway's existence now remains. To the south, the formation remains visible from the air. As does the Prestleigh Inn – seen in the bottom left corner of the picture!

The line continues south from the site of the former Prestleigh Viaduct, still descending at 1 in 50. The trackbed itself is more discernible and it is interesting to note the typical use made of the formation to provide accessible agricultural storage facilities. The Royal Bath and West of England Showground stands out clearly although its appearance can change dramatically when in use. At the top right of the shot is the grey farm storage building previously mentioned as a guide in tracking the line north towards Cannards Grave.

Evercreech New Station

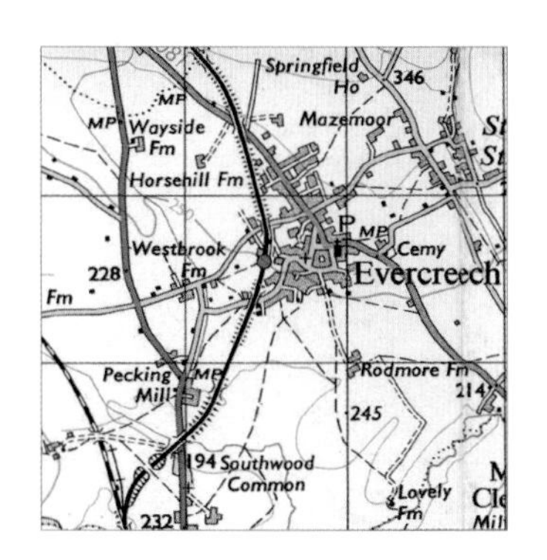

ABOVE Line histories, photographic collections and reminiscences all highlight the importance and operational working of Evercreech Junction. However, this station wasn't as convenient for accessing the town from which it takes its name. Evercreech New, some 1¾ miles further north, was situated on a sweeping curve to the west side of the substantial village. In the picture the camera faces south with the line appearing from the bottom of the shot, crossing the B3081 and passing between the village and Leighton Lane industrial estate. As with so much of the railway's former infrastructure, once more virtually all has been swept aside.

FACING PAGE Evercreech New station handled both milk and lime traffic in addition to the normal goods services for the village. Modern housing now occupies the station site. Tracing the line past the industrial estate, Leighton Lane can be seen crossing at right angles. Just beyond, the green field to the right of the trackbed has a line of trees pointing towards the village and roughly at the station site itself. All that now remains is a single stone abutment on the northern side of the former bridge crossing Leighton Lane, and two further stone abutments on the crossing of Pecking Mill Road to the south of the station site. Given that the industrial estate is now home to a multinational company distributing dairy products, how convenient the railway and its goods yard would now be had it survived!

No 53808 is in charge of the 10 coaches of the 10.40am Exmouth to Cleethorpes SO on Saturday 11 August 1962 and makes its steady way through Evercreech New. The '7F' took over the train at Templecombe Upper for the journey over the Mendips to Bath and now faces 8 miles at a ruling gradient of 1 in 50 to Masbury Summit.

Pecking Mill Viaduct

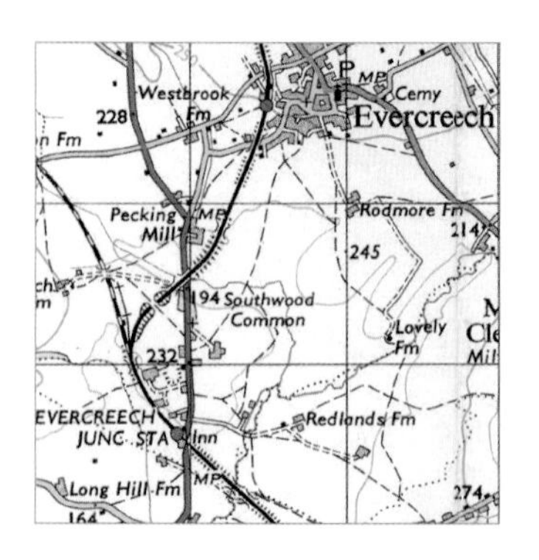

ABOVE Having departed Evercreech New, down trains now crossed the A371 just prior to slowing for the 25mph speed restriction for Pecking Mill Curve. At this point the Highbridge branch joined at Evercreech Junction and the line ran on towards the station itself. The remains of Pecking Mill Viaduct can be seen in the left corner of this wider aerial view of the Evercreech Junction site.

FACING PAGE Formerly a five-span structure, the central spans straddling the A371 have been demolished leaving just the supporting brickwork at either side of the road. Once again the growth of lineside vegetation means that today's traveller may well have sped past the remnants of the viaduct without even registering its presence!

Evercreech Junction

ABOVE The final destination for this part of the journey south from Bath is Evercreech Junction, opened as Evercreech in 1862 but renamed in 1874 to avoid confusion with the aptly named Evercreech New on the Bath extension. It was an important and well known station on the line; all freights and virtually every passenger train stopped here to take on water, attach or detach pilot engines, or both. Down trains from Bath were forced to slow to 25mph for Pecking Mill curve, still clearly visible in this shot. This approach was in contrast with the line from Highbridge. Being the original line, this enjoyed the benefits of a straighter alignment which also stands out from above as the darker patch on the brown field. The A371 runs down the left hand side of the picture with the actual station site falling just by the point at which the railway crossed the road by means of a level crossing.

FACING PAGE Immediately to the left of the crossing, the former Railway Hotel still stands and has been renamed as 'The Natterjack'. The original station building can be seen on the former down platforms and is occupied as private dwellings. All other railway infrastructure has disappeared, including the large water tank formerly situated to the south of the road and which featured in many pictures of Evercreech Junction.

Friday 4 March 1966 was the last weekday of operation of the emergency passenger service following the postponement of the intended January 1966 closure. No 76005 pulls the stock of the 3.30pm Templecombe to Evercreech Junction over the crossover before reversing it into the down platform for the 4.13pm departure for Bournemouth. Few of the drivers waiting on the A371 road crossing are going to regret the closure of the line!

No 41296 has just arrived at Evercreech Junction on Easter Monday 19 April 1965 with a train from Highbridge consisting of a single coach and a utility van. Much to the frustration of drivers on the A371, the level crossing gates are closed to road traffic while the train awaits the right away for its onward journey to Templecombe.

Taken from the east, this view shows the amount of redevelopment that has taken place on the site since the railway was closed and the tracks lifted. As a junction with the Highbridge and Burnham branches, Evercreech saw a considerable amount of traffic; there were no less than three sets of goods sidings (including the station goods yard) and shunting was a 24-hour activity. This bustling railway outpost has now disappeared, replaced by light industrial and storage units to the extent that, once again, the former track formation can only be truly appreciated from the air.

It is Whit Monday 18 May 1964 and, with this Bath to Bournemouth excursion and a following Bristol to Bournemouth excursion, Bath MPD has been reduced to producing No 48660 to pilot 73049 over the Mendips. The reporting number has already been removed from the pilot to the train engine as it is being uncoupled. Despite an 18-minute late departure from Bath, arrival at Bournemouth West was 18 minutes early in an overall time of 2 hours 19 minutes.

FACING PAGE The camera now looks down towards the site of the former level crossing which took the line across the A371. Immediately beyond the crossing several of the original station buildings are still standing and in private use. The station suffered from being built on a ruling gradient of 1 in 105 which meant that up trains faced an uphill start on their assault of the Mendips. One of the siding bufferstops was even fitted with a three-link coupling to prevent goods wagons running away downhill through station limits! A centre siding between the running lines in the station itself was used for repositioning the branchline stock between mainline trains and, in summer months, held up to five locomotives waiting to pilot heavy trains north on the climb to Masbury summit. Although road traffic was lighter than today, the delays caused by the level crossing in the summer must have been frustrating for motorists not enthralled by railway operations!

OVERLEAF One building that can be traced back through previous photographic studies of the line is the original station building which now sports a more modern conservatory extension. Dating back to 1862 and the days of the Somerset Central Railway, it was enlarged and converted into the stationmaster's house when the extension to Bath was completed. The trackbed has been infilled and motorists speed past unhindered and probably unaware of the significance of the former junction station.

LEFT From height the beauty of the countryside through which the Somerset & Dorset railway ran can be truly appreciated. Although only 26 track miles from Bath Road Junction, the nature of the line has varied from the picturesque Midford valley, to the Radstock coalfields and finally the rolling Somerset landscape south of the Mendips. As a reminder of the journey through previous pages, Evercreech Junction sits at the bottom of the picture. The line can be traced back past Evercreech New to the right, the Royal Bath and West Showground at midpoint, with Shepton Mallet just visible above. The Mendip Hills sit in the distance, providing a reminder of the challenges faced by railwaymen in operating this remarkable and much missed line.

HATTERJACK